First published in Great Britain in 2021

ISBN 978-1-7399694-0-0

Written, edited, designed and illustrated by Camilla Werdelin

Layout by Julie Werdelin

when the tide leaves you bare

To all the brave and beautiful people who have journeyed with me, fought with me, and fought for me.

This book is for you.

Prologue

i remember what it used to be like. i remember being so hungry that i didn't even know what hunger was anymore. i remember the guilt a strawberry held. i remember how my heart would plummet into my stomach as i was faced with a meal and how a thousand thoughts would fly through my mind about how i could possibly approach, or better, avoid it. how i would hear nothing but my own mind. how my feet ached but i couldn't stop walking. how i was locked in a world where nothing made sense and yet it was the only one i understood. and oh, how to get out. how was there possibly a way out? it was all under control but i had no control. i fought against everyone but i had no fight to get myself out. i didn't even know where to start. people were telling me but i had already decided it was hopeless.

but that was the thing, i had not decided. i hadn't decided anything. i hadn't decided this life and i hadn't decided to be stuck. it was an illness inflicted upon me and yet the very mind that was sick was the only mind that could get me well.

but there were other minds too. thank god for other minds. people who put their heads together to help me find the person that was deep inside me who knew she wanted a better life.

the control had to be re-directed. the control had to be re-wired into my arms that lifted the fork up to my mouth. the fear had to be found in the possibility of being stuck like this forever. the questions had to be asked about what was underneath. the trauma had to be unearthed. the thousands of thoughts and feelings and words had to fall out into my writing and my art instead of onto my body.

everything that made me sick was also everything that got me well. it was hard and painful and exhausting. but day by day i re-routed myself onto a better path. and soon i didn't have to think so hard. soon it became what i intuitively wanted. my body told me what it wanted and i allowed myself to listen. and i slowly woke up. i was awake. i was breathing. i was crying and i was aching but i was breathing and i was healing. i came back. you can always come back. but you have to want to find home. you have to want to find yourself.

here i lay,
open,
bare and broken,
the storm cleansed me
of all superficial.
i am nothing
but my words and i.
this is me,
finding my home,
this is what happens,
when the storm is over,
this is who you are,
when the tide leaves you bare.

when the tide leaves you bare

September 2019, Warwick

there are always these story books about children who are misunderstood and lonely, but then turn out to be special and unique, and the world finally sees them. i think i used to deeply hope, and tell myself, that that was me. that one day i would do something that would make up for - i don't know - everything i was lacking.

October 2019, Warwick

stop playing around. this isn't a game. this is your life. and you're about to let it all go. i don't know where you're going to find that hope, that fight, but you have to find it. please.

October 2019, Warwick

i think it's always thought that secrets make you more lonely, and they do. but they also make you feel less alone. because when you're alone, it's not just you. it's you and your secrets.

November 2019, London

i have to remember that if no one had intervened all those years ago, i would not be here today. that illness would have killed me, one way or another. and as much as i hate to see it or accept it, it's that same illness i'm engaging with now.

i know no one will come along and save me. that's the painful truth, but i feel like deep down that hope is still alive. it almost feels too painful to save myself, because it's a reminder of all the times i wanted saving and no one was there, and how i fear that that's still the case today, and will be for the rest of my life.

the sea

go into the wild and find what you need …

Belonging

Trust

Love

Compassion

Courage

Understanding

Safety

Care

Hope

i need

i need water to drink,
i need food to eat,
the sun for light,
fire for heat.

i need kind people, kind words,
a hand to hold,
someone to listen,
to stories untold.

i need faith and trust,
the courage to fight fear,
when struggle and darkness,
feel far too near.

i need the fight to keep going,
hope, for every new day,
and above everything, i need to know,
that to need is okay.

January 2020, London

i am being held hostage inside my own mind.

things to remember

first of all, remember you don't need to hide. your world isn't going to fall apart if you let someone see who you are. those parts of you, you think should never be seen, are the ones most in need of love. remember that emotions aren't dangerous, they are a beautiful and essential part of feeling alive. remember that life is best without rules, and that some of the greatest things come out of uncertainty and change.

remember that the sun makes everything better. that nothing is permanent. that everything always feels better once you wake up. remember that the sea makes you feel alive, and the stars can make darkness a beautiful thing. that the feeling of grass on your feet connects you to the earth and that you are an integral part of this life as much as anyone else.

remember that people don't always want something from you. that some people are there for you just because they care. and that those people are worth holding onto. remember that people sometimes disappoint you, but if it's meant to be, it can always be fixed.

but most of all, remember that you are a person. not a defective version of a person. but a human being who deserves what every human being deserves. people who love you. who laugh with you. hope that things get better. kindness. in everything. the sun kissing your face. babies smiling at you. a break. when things get too hard. a hug to get you back on your feet.

so with this, take another step forward. another step towards hope. life isn't always beautiful, but there is always beauty in life.

February 2020, London

i'm not dying,
so i must be ok?
no
i am not ok
i am on the edge of a cliff
i'm scared and i'm tired
will this ever end?

listen to the whispers

there must be a part that loves,
that took me where i am today,
that when everything felt broken,
whispered quietly to say,
'you don't need to be alone,
you don't need to be at war,
when you feel like you might be drowning,
keep swimming,
you'll find the shore'

it will all be okay

like little children,
we look around,
trying to find the next person
who will love us.
wanting to be held, picked up
when the world feels a little too big.
wrapped up in warm safe hands,
head resting against a soft chest,
listening to the heart that loves you,
beating to the mellow sounds of
'it will all be ok'.
then one day that heart became
your own.
the world became bigger, and the
hands once held felt smaller, less safe,
less soft.
yet that heart remains.
wait quietly, as you listen to that
mellow sound,
beating,
it will all be ok.

pandemic

and the world quietens,
comes to a rest,
mothers and fathers come home,
we return to the nest,
so much fear and worry,
for what the future will hold,
no one knows how,
this tale could unfold.
there are tears and anger,
when we utter goodbyes,
as chapters close,
on too many lives.
the rest of us are locked
inside as a nation,
oh the stories we'll tell
the next generation.

March 2020, London

i think so much of what was keeping me stuck, was fear about life and about what could happen, and about not wanting to see how terrible it could be.

whereas right now, i feel like the worst has happened. if you asked me what would be the worst thing that could happen to the world, it would be something like this.

and it's happening and we're getting through it, it's hard and it's scary, but people are coming together and we're not alone. we're getting through it. so maybe i can get through everything else there is to come.

isolation

when everything was falling apart,
i longed for answers,
a way out of the lost and broken,
and someone always knew,
what to say, where to go,
there was always a chance,
a future to long for,
others seeing the light,
shouting 'come this way!'.
yes i was alone,
and i longed for people to
live in my world,
just for a day,
where distances are vast,
the sun an artificial hope,
a new day is just the same,
and all is unknown.
but now i miss that loneliness,
for now everyone lives here.
there are no more answers,
we are all blind,
and no one knows where to be or go,
who to trust.
i long for a hug,
but we cannot touch.
and comforting words are lost,
when no one believes them.
my isolation was once mine,
but now it is everywhere,
on every face i see.
and it is not comforting.

May 2020, London

i sometimes think why was i so damaged by my experiences? because they're not unique.

September 2021, Denmark - response

you were hurt. and that's all that matters.

May 2020, London

let yourself be held. breathe. you weren't meant to navigate this world alone. that's not what living is for. there are people out there who want to know you. who want to see you. for all the intricacy of love and fear and imperfection that you are. those pieces that don't quite seem to fit, let them see light. you don't need to keep half of yourself in darkness. let yourself love, just so that your heart can break. let yourself be loved, just so you can feel the depth of never wanting them to leave. because that is to truly feel. live. it's the only way. break. cry. feel. fall apart. come back together. come home to who you are. there is no way to make it through life without pain. but that is what love is for. what connection is for. to hold each other through darkness. and to be there when the light returns.

May 2020, London

if not now, when?

May 2020, London

who stops you from speaking?
made sharing forbidden?
the world didn't ask you
to keep your words hidden.

May 2020, London

you are stuck, not broken

June 2020, London

coming back to where you started is not the same thing as never leaving.

you

you are not your past,
the hurt you hold,
you are not the stories,
you've left untold.
you are not the words
you said in fear,
you are not the pain
you felt that year.
you are not the tears,
you keep inside,
you are not the thoughts
you've learned to hide.
you are the star that shines,
on a lonely night,
you are the storm that never
gives up the fight.
you are the dreams you've held
through all the years,
you are the gentle courage
in all the tears.
you are each time
you touched another's soul
you are the other half
of someone's whole.
so keep holding on
for life to show,
you are so much more
than you could ever know.

H.old O.n P.ain E.nds

when all seems lost,
and each tear falls,
packaged with fear, loss, loneliness,
or maybe it all,
maybe the end feels far,
the journey too long,
each step too tiresome,
too tired to hold on.
but something awakens,
to hold you through,
each dark lonely night,
you pray that it's true,
that happiness survives,
and hope will descend,
breathe, this will pass,
hold on, pain ends.

my house

i used to watch the sky melt
honey yellow into blue,
mimic the birds in their path,
dancing gently as they flew,

i never questioned how the world
turned every day to night,
never feared if darkness really
would make space for light.

but as the years came on, i
replaced the trust with an ache,
mornings kept on coming, but
myself i couldn't wake,

the world still just as dark,
as left the day before,
walking blindly in a life,
that felt like home no more.

i reached out an empty hand,
but found only lonely air,
so i built myself a house to live
when no one else was there.

a wall for each time
i let someone hurt my heart,
a wall for each time i broke,
each time i fell apart.

but the more i built the walls,
the less i looked outside,
and when visitors came knocking
i would take my heart and hide,

and though the sun kept rising,
there was safety in the dark,
the only way i knew, to keep
the hurt from my heart.

but just like leaves use the light
to know which way to grow,
when cracks appeared in the walls,
the child from long ago,

reached out her hand one more time,
to see what she would find,
leaping back, when what she met was
something warm and kind.

and more months passed in the dark,
shivering on my own,
but every time i reached through,
i found i wasn't alone.

and after all the lonely years
i'd kept myself locked up inside,
keeping all myself unseen and
all my tears un-cried,

the garden outside my house had grown,
with yellow light beaming down,
and though my heart was fearful,
there were people all around,

showing me what light can do,
if you let it in,
and so i started breaking down
the walls from deep within.

my knuckles bled and bruised,
as i fought with every wall,
often sinking to the ground,
but getting up to see them fall,

and the more light flooded in,
the more i stood up to the fight,
at first it hurt my eyes, but there
was beauty in the light.

beauty in the hurting child
coming out of hiding,
beauty in the tears that come
when children start confiding,

and though my house kept me safe
from people, loss and pain,
the garden only grew with both
the light and with the rain,

so here i plant my heart again,
to weather the unknown,
trying to trust that here is safe,
and through it all, i've grown.

maybe wounds don't stain

maybe, if you looked inside,
there would be nothing left to see,
no marks left behind,
just a plain old version of me.
maybe wounds don't stain,
maybe hurt doesn't defeat,
maybe my lungs just want to breathe,
and my heart just wants to beat.

June 2020, London

held by soft grass and people that feel like flowers.

August 2020, Denmark

sometimes i wonder if i keep quiet, not because i don't have anything to say, but because there is too much.

maybe there's more than what has gone by

i guess i tend to think i am a collection
of difficult times gone by,
each chapter stored away in corners,
and no matter how much i try,
i can't starve the stories of oxygen,
and they take a life of their own,
reaching up and out to be heard,
when i find myself alone.
so i prefer to make myself a number,
turn pain into grades and grams,
but lately i've been thinking,
maybe that's not all that i am.
i am the sunrise over danish seas,
pink water mirrored in my eyes,
i am the laughter shared with those i love
under the yellowing skies,
i am the shock of cold against my skin,
as i leap into the morning sea,
i am the memories of dancing in the grass,
singing wild and free.
i am the hands that hold my sisters when
they reach up for a hug,
i am the eyes that watch the bonfire burn
wrapping blankets around me snug.
and maybe it is all these things,
that will slowly take up my mind,
the space that these memories take
will push the darkness aside.
for life is more than what has happened,
it is everything that is to come,
so i will stay to see how life unfolds,
to see everything more i become.

and i grow

eternal winter

silencing yourself,
is like telling a tree to grow without producing its
leaves,
and while every other tree turns from brown to green
in the warmth,
you are stuck in an eternal winter.

September 2020, London

i can't believe i've made it through. so much has happened, i can look at my life and think i'm not where i'd like to be or where i feel i should be, but really, i have changed more in the past six months than ever. who i am, how i see myself in terms of who i really am, not who i thought i was or who i felt i needed to be, and letting myself be that. letting myself be messy, spilling out, allowing people to see me spill and fall apart, and experiencing being held in ways i thought was not possible, in moments i thought no one would ever be able to meet me in. i've been my loudest and my quietest, loved in both places. my happiest and saddest, and cared for equally in it all. i've seen things break, and watched things heal, things i never thought could heal. i made it through. we made it through. i've watched people fight for their lives through unreal circumstances, and as much as i don't believe it, i think i have too. it has floored me how much the heart will always fight for it's human.

i am homesick for a place
i have not yet found.

but i am longing.

and with longing comes hope.

September 2020, London

find me in the stormy seas,
peering out through broken tears,
fingers tightly curled round the mast,
dancing in the wind like that of an old birch tree.

September 2020, London

i would much rather have you at your worst,

than never have you at all.

the storm

October 2020, London

one day you wake up and you find yourself here.
in a life you don't recognise. and nothing makes sense.
how did you get from that to this?
you used to paint flowers on mothers-day cards.

shelter

lay low, and close,
curl up against the wind.
close your eyes, and rest,
and trust.
remember the little one,
sleeping still in your heart,
that you would tell her
there is no shame in waiting.
and when the darkness passes,
lift your head up,
brush knotted hair from your lips,
turn your eyes to the sky.
the sun will come out again,
the sounds of the storm will mellow,
your feet will find the earth,
and onwards we go.

October 2020, London

you reached down inside me,
and took out my heart,
you held it in your hands,
and picked each piece apart
you kept those you needed,
and left the others behind,
and now there is nothing
but loneliness inside.

stay wild

when the wind is strong,
and the clouds are dark,
go into the wild,
and plant your heart.
surrender to rain,
the frost and snow,
for despite every winter,
you will grow.
again and again,
you'll survive the dark,
no matter how cold,
or harsh or stark.
you will survive,
through every weather,
no matter the pain,
it's never forever,
and if there one thing i wish,
i'd been told as a child,
it will always be,
do not fear the wild.

November 2020, London

i know you are having a difficult time right now,
sometimes you feel lost,
sometimes you feel overwhelmed by the world,
sometimes you feel like you don't belong,
sometimes you feel like you're never going to be able
to figure it out.
but i am here to tell you
that you are loved,
that you are held,
that the world needs you,
even when you are sad,
even when you are angry,
even when you are quiet,
the world needs you.
and one day you will feel that warmth,
and you will find your place here again,
and you will root your feet into the earth,
and call it your home.

November 2020, London

maybe you don't need to spend your whole life searching for the 'meaning' of it all. maybe you don't need that definite reason or purpose you feel so lost without. every day, you wake up and choose to be alive. notice that. you are still here, reading this page, because you chose to be. when you feel hopeless, you are not all hopelessness. a sliver of hope is keeping you here, still. you don't always need a reason for living. sometimes just the quiet knowing of 'i want to live' is enough.

it's been a year

it's been a year,
of turmoil and tears,
finding myself among
new hopes and fears.

it's been a year,
of letting people in,
to see the darkness
and sadness within.

it's been a year,
of feeling free,
to be who i am,
and letting them see.

it's been a year,
of holding my friends,
echoing 'i'll stay,
right through till the end'.

it's been a year,
of letting them hold me,
when my heart felt empty,
and helping me see,

that it's been a year,
and it's easy to say,
why aren't you done?
why aren't you okay?

but it's been a year,
and the critics in my mind,
are slowly learning,
that it's better to be kind.

so it's been a year,
and now i know,
there is no timeline for
healing, and through
everything, we grow.

November 2020, London

fuck you, anorexia. i am so much more than what you tried to shrink me into.

let me go

11pm comes
it's time for bed
but wait a minute
what was it she said?
or was it my fault
did i say something wrong?
there's no reply to my message
oh it's been way too long.
midnight passes
i'm 7 years old
i'm thinking about the time
i was stupidly bold
oh and all the mistakes
i ever have made
and that job last year
was i ever paid?
it's 2am now
i am losing my mind
who cares what i lost?
it's sleep i can't find
and all the thoughts go
around and around
like a washing machine
that just won't slow down.
the night gets more lonely
as i lie there awake
i'm thinking if i have
medication to take.
eventually my thoughts
quiet down into sleep,
until tomorrow night comes,
where it all will repeat.

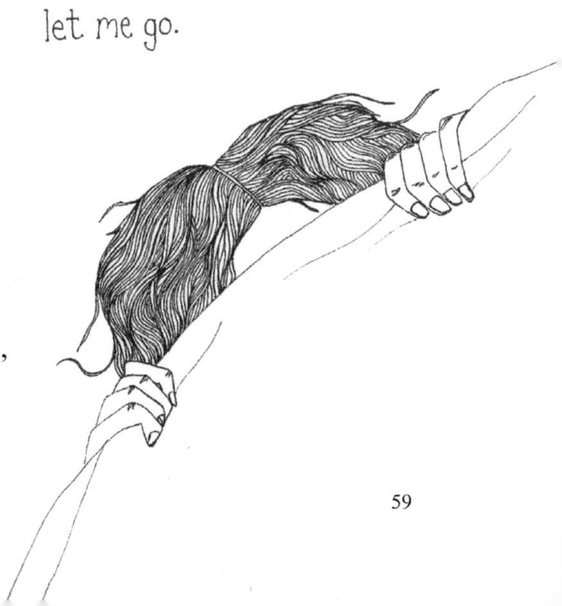

December 2020, Oxford

lean into the storm,
for it never meant to hurt you.
the wind is merely showing you
which way you're supposed to go.

silence is not my song anymore

i ache
for the hurt you
imposed upon me.
and i try to
be brave.
but clouds can only
hold so much
before they rain.

and i pour.
finally.
for silence is not
my song
anymore.

i ache
for the hurt you
imposed upon me.
but i will rain,
i will pour,
until i am empty
of your darkness.
for it does not
belong with me.
it is not mine.

it is yours.
it belongs
with you.

and i will not
carry it
anymore.

December 2020, Oxford

you have time. be patient with yourself. if you needed that extra year to become who you wanted to be, that's okay.

the sea always had you

you may feel alone,
adrift out at sea,
the world unknown,
fears running free,
like no one is watching
your little boat sail,
and if the waves got too big,
your boat would fail.
but you must trust the
journey,
for storms always end,
the waves will come
crashing,
but you can depend,
on your heart and your
strength
for you were never alone.

the sea always had you,
just the wind that had blown,
had made little waves
look tsunamis to you,
but when the wind calms
the light will come through,
and your boat will go on,
your strength still alive,
and a breath you'll exhale,
for the storm you survived.

missing is a kind of suffocating

nothing compares to the pain of missing something so much, you think you may never come up for air. but there is too much air, empty air, that should be filled with what was once there. the saddest thing about it all, is that you must keep breathing. you cannot stop it. the empty air must fill your lungs, and run through your blood, and you will feel the emptiness run through you.

it will be painful. and it will feel different and unknown. but the air that is so painful, is the same air that will keep your heart beating and your lungs breathing, it is what will keep you alive. and alive is hope. you will survive. as long as you keep breathing, you will survive. and with time it will become less painful. one day, each breath won't hurt as much.

hope for the time to come

and she is wild.
she dances in the rain,
embracing the soft touch,
of droplets falling over her skin.
as she turns into the sky,
she closes her eyes,
and settles in the
afternoon light.
and now she smiles,
for the tears that lay
on her face today,
are those of a new life.
the sky washes away,
the fear that has lived,
for far too long
inside her.
and she can finally breathe.
the light scent
of hope and promise.
for now, she is free.

on a moonlit night, a young girl steps out onto an empty beach. she falls to her knees with heaviness, and the water rushes up to meet her. she looks out at the vast emptiness, and it stirs something inside her, and slowly the tears she has been holding so tightly, glide gently down to meet the sea. and she aches, for all that is lost. the tears start pouring out, like rain, and the ache becomes deeper, taking root in her heart, and it feels as though parts of her are withering away. she is afraid. afraid of her heart, afraid of her soul, afraid of the pain, the loss, the loneliness, afraid it will never stop.

but slowly, she starts to feel the warm, soft sand engulfing her fingers. the wind that gently lifts her hair with each breath. she feels the sea lightly wrap itself around her legs and her heart beat in it's gentle rhythm. she lifts her head up, and her eyes open to see everything that lies before her. her tears slowly come to a rest, and she breathes out heavily. and in that moment she realises the ache has quietened. the pain, the loss, the loneliness, it left her in her tears. for this is what her body had been waiting for all this time.

~ *what she was most afraid of was the thing she needed most.*

the gallery

my life is a museum i often walk,
with many pictures across the walls,
and i often hold my breath as i wonder,
through the crowded gallery halls.
for when i stop to take a look,
i never know what i will see,
i might recognise a moment of joy,
or see an unwelcome memory.
some are beautiful collections,
of azure skies and laughter,
some are dark and lonely,
that i would never return to after.
some are puzzles with pieces lost,
and i can't make them make sense,
some i know so accurately,
and the feelings are much too intense.
sometimes i wish i could leave the museum,
or i feel i can't find my way through,
for life is long, and the museum is big,
and i want to replace the old with the new.
but my favourite part of these visits,
is the pictures of all those i love,
the smiles of those who are here with me now,
or those who are watching me from up above.
for despite the darkness and lonely i see,
there are three more paintings of light,
and despite the pictures that frighten me,
there are many more where i stand up and fight.
so next time i take this walk i'll remember,
how there is a certain delicate beauty,
in seeing these paintings of love and of loss,
and how it is all of them, that set me free.

fairytale

pick up your sword,
and face the fight,
the dragons will come,
but you'll face the fright,
many demons you'll slay,
along the way,
but you'll get up again,
to fight each day.
you'll put on your armour,
run into the wild,
and all of the children,
you will inspire.
for in this story,
you always win,
you wrote it yourself,
it exists within.

conversations with my inner child

i want to write a letter,
to the child i used to be,
before the world became so big
and i was young and free.
i want to tell her she is brave,
for trying all that she tries,
i want to tell her she is seen,
even if sometimes she hides.
i want to tell her she is loved,
by people far and wide,
i want to tell her she is strong,
even if sometimes she cries.
i want to tell her she is never forgotten,
that she is always held in mind,
i want to tell her people feel
how her heart is warm and kind.
i want to tell her she can face,
all that comes her way,
i want to tell her she has inside,
all she needs to face each day.
i want to tell her i am proud,
for all she came to be,
for now i can hold my head up high,
and say that little girl was me.

poisonous shame. it starts in your heart, and then it pumps out with every beat, through your arteries and into the corners of your body. it sits there and seeps into your skin, and over time you forget where it started, and it becomes part of your being, forgetting that once upon a time it did not belong to you, you were once you without it. you believe it is so inherently part of you that you chose to keep parts of yourself in darkness, you silence yourself. the problem is that if you always hide it, you will never see that you can be seen as all of you, and still be wanted, still be loved, still held close. because the mistake you made was that the shame was never meant to make a home within you. and now it is time to open the windows, let the heavy air out, and let the lightness in, and it is time to breath. you were never meant for shame. and we knew it all along.

~ i always knew that shame was not for you

we will love again

here we are again.
crying on the pages,
tears patterned between words
as i write out my labyrinthine heart.
who knows how long i've been here,
it could be days, months, years
for sadness knows no end
and apparently nor does love.
for it is love falling out of me,
in every silken drop,
i heard it was called heartbreak,
but i never understood,
how you could feel your heart
tearing apart
with every searing breath,
and it seems unfair
that such an ethereal emotion,
is so tightly wound in pain.
but that is who we humans are
we will love again
and again.

my rebellion

pretty girls,
with perfect hair,
never argue,
never stare,
you must be quiet,
you must be nice,
you must walk softly,
quiet as mice.
you must be kind,
you must be clever,
achieve those grades,
you must be better.
follow the rules,
never rest,
you must always strive,
to be the best.
never gossip,
never fight,
always be happy,
smiley and bright.
shall we carry on?
there's an endless list,
of all the things,
you've sorely missed.
hang on a minute.
what am i saying?
fuck the system,
fuck the obeying,
fuck your opinions,
fuck all of your rules,
i'm going to unlearn
what you taught us at school.
i want to get out,
i want to be free,
i want to be brave,
i want to be me,
i want to run,
into the wild,
and play hide and seek,
with myself as a child.
there'll be no more silence,
i'll scream and i'll shout,
so everyone knows,
what i am about.
i'll eat what i want,
and i won't brush my hair,
for i've got better things to do,
and i really don't care.
and when the day is done,
i'll crawl into bed,
and i won't obsess,
over everything i've said.
for my fire is burning,
my match is lit,
for i am finally done with
taking everyone's shit.

how to heal the world

if only i could make
the things i feel
would help this hurting
world to heal.

i'd bring all of the love
from all of the mothers
and spread it across
every sister and brother.

i'd grow all the forests
falling over with green,
so the life source we breath
could be pure and clean.

i'd stop all the smoke
that is heating our air
so the icebergs won't melt
and we save the white bear.

i'd replace all of the anger
that brings war to our land,
with the strength in our
children, to take a brave
stand.

i'd make all schools teach
lessons, in love and in fears,
so children don't feel shame,
when they show us their tears.

i'd tell all girls and boys
they are beautiful as they are,
that happiness and love
can be felt from afar.

i'd heal all of our hearts,
empty out the despair,
fill each pocket with love,
stitch us together with care.

we wish we were made of moon and stars

i'll take a breath
and i'll accept,
the parts of me
i've often kept,
hidden inside
so i wouldn't see,
the things i didn't
want in me.
deep inside,
they've quietly slept,
but when they'd awake,
up i'd be swept,
as now is their time
to show who they are,
as they finally break
the prison bars.
but if i didn't
try to hide,
or keep them squashed
so deep inside,
maybe they'll slowly
learn to see,
that they can find
a friend in me.
and maybe i'll
be less afraid,
and maybe they'll
feel less betrayed,
and from the prison
they'll be released,
and we can live
in tender peace.
for we all have parts
we wish weren't ours,
we wish we were made
of moon and stars,
but messy we are
not tidy and neat,
and in this embrace
we become complete.

February 2021, London

i don't have a plan. i have no idea where i am going. every day i can wake up, and i can choose to stew on this fact, anxiously try to think, think, think my way through to a future that is impossible to create, because none of us, however much we think we have a plan, can know what it entails.

or i can chose to wake up every day, and breath a sigh of relief that i don't have a plan. i can go wherever i want to. meet whomever i want to spend time with. see new places or stay in the same. go on adventures if i'm feeling sunny, or curl myself up dry from the rain. travelling through life is like travelling through vietnam on a bus. i will need to buy several bus tickets. but i only need to buy one at a time. i only need to know where i am going, one place at a time.

and then i can rest and listen to myself - where do i want to go next? or do i want to stay here? who do i want to go with? what do i want to let go of?

life is made up of hundreds, thousands of small trips, from one place to the next. some are longer, more arduous, and some are short and beautiful. there are infinite routes. infinite combinations. how exciting to live in a life where anything can happen. having no plan is the best plan of all.

stay

i must stay for the dreams,
for the golden sun.
i must stay for the stars,
count them, one by one.
i must stay for the sea,
to be held by the waves,
i must stay for the light,
every day it saves.
i must stay for the love,
every soft embrace.
i must stay for the strength,
for the days we face.
i must stay for the tears,
we share with each other,
i must stay for the truth,
that we show one another.
i must stay for the peace,
as into slumber i fall,
i must stay for this life,
i must stay for it all.

February 2021, London

it always gets better.
all the times you thought it wouldn't and then it did.
it always gets better.
no amount of human strength can stop the sun from rising,
just like no amount of darkness can stop the light from rising within you.
it will always get better.
it always does.
hold on.

your fight

be proud of your scars,
the battles you've fought,
the words you've spoken,
the help you've sought.
be proud of the days,
you made it through,
when the end of the tunnel,
was far from view.
be proud of the times,
you let people in,
to see the truth,
you held within.
be proud of yourself
for everything you do,
for the person you need,
she's here, she's you.

the children need us

growing up i always knew,
there were many things i shouldn't do,
many things were taught in school,
to follow every way and rule.

and although i'm glad i know to be kind,
and i know how to make the most of my mind,
there are many more things that children need,
much more than learning how to succeed.

children need a helping hand,
to be brave enough to take a stand,
to be able to say enough is enough,
when children start to play too rough.

they need to learn to scream and shout,
if danger starts to come about,
they need to know that although they are small,
they should never be tripped and left to fall.

they need to know if they get lost,
someone will find them at any cost,
they need to know that they are seen,
that if they are hurt we'll intervene.

they need to know that they are adored,
even if they don't win an award,
they need to know that they can expect,
that adults will always come to protect.

and above everything else children should know,
they are loved no matter how much they grow,
and we will fight until we see,
that this world is a warm and safe place to be.

March 2021, London

you did today. and maybe you didn’t do that much today, maybe you feel no closer to where you want to be. but you survived today, you showed up, and as insignificant as it may feel, you grew a little more today.

March 2021, London

you are so needed here. don’t give up. the world is waiting to show you all of its beauty, and for you to show it all of yours.

i need no one more than myself

i thought i needed you
i thought i needed you to be okay
i needed you to tell me i was good
that i was perfect
that i could be just like you
if i tried better.

i never realised the control you had on me
that subtle kind of control
that doesn't even feel like anything.
the invisible power someone has
when they convince you it is your brain
that is telling you the wrong things
not them.
that it's your trust issues
it's your insecurity
it's your problem.

do you realise the damage
of convincing someone
their own selves are untrustworthy?

but i am healing now
after years out of your grip
i can finally see,

it's your trust issues
it's your insecurity
it's your problem.
i am on my side,
you were not.

and i can take back the control now
and vow to never,
let someone convince me,
that i need someone else
more than i need myself.

Helen
- for Eleanor

how to explain,
a love that is lost,
when you would bring something back,
no matter the cost.
just for one night,
to fall asleep to your song,
to be held in your arms,
back where i belong.
but i still long for sleep,
even when you're not there,
for in these midnight hours,
the world becomes fair,
and you haven't been taken,
so suddenly away,
in my dreams you live with me,
but in my dreams you will stay.
how to explain,
a love that is taken,
that leaves families broken,
forsaken and shaken,
but it is in the rising,
the crying, the breaking,
the breathing, the loosing,
the finding, the aching,
there is the love,
that i can't explain,
it is forever inside me,
among all the pain,
and when i fall asleep,
i'll find you somewhere,
for in my dreams you will stay,
and you will always be there.

what will i tell my children?

what will i tell my daughters?
when they are no longer little girls,
when their eyes are painted darker,
and their face is framed with curls.
do i tell them to be careful,
when they are walking down the street,
do i tell them to be quiet,
walk in groups and be discreet.
even when i am a mother,
will i still have to think,
to watch my glass at night,
in case they spike my drink?
what will i tell my sons?
when they are no longer little boys,
when they prefer to watch the football,
instead of playing with their toys,
do i tell them to be careful,
of the talk they'll hear as men,
that humour is much more sinister,
than it was when they were ten.
even when i am a mother,
will i still have to think,
my boys might scare the girls,
when they come in for a drink?
i hope this is the last
generation where the norm,
is that girls are dainty flowers,
and boys are the storm.
i hope we pave the way,
to the world we want to see,
where girls are not the victim,
and boys stay young and free.

March 2021, London

what is the self?
what if everything that had happened to you had never happened?
who would you be left with?

what are you seeing?

body

this is my body,
this is my home,
my place to be,
my house to roam.
but when it is changing,
where do i go?
do i dare to stay?
or do i forego,
the home that has held me
through all of my years,
the heart that has held
all my worries and fears,
the mind that has mended
when broken and weak,
has held me together
when weary and meek.
through all of the starving,
and making it thin,
despite all the harming,
it never gave in.
so do i desert it?
when i don't like what i see?
do i deny
what it needs to be me?

how can i hate
a body of healing,
a body of protection,
a body of feeling?
after all these years,
i will finally allow,
my body to be loved,
and from here on i vow,
i will protect you
through all of our living,
i will give back the love,
you have always been
giving.

April 2021, London

i don't believe everything happens for a reason. but i believe everything happens to show you something. the loss of someone shows you how much love you are capable of feeling. the worst days show you how much you can face and still survive. the sadness shows you that you wish for better for yourself. the anger shows you that you know what is right and wrong. the pain shows you you are a living, breathing, feeling human being. and that you are capable of healing.

sister lessons

to my dear little sisters,
how much i would tell you,
about this great big world
you are growing into.
there are so many things
i wish i had known,
when i was half my age,
just barely grown.
i wish i had known
that no matter the rain,
the sun would always come back
to see me again,
and when i say rain,
i mean the rain clouds hide,
but also the rain
that pours inside.
i wish i had known
that some people stay,
but some people go,
and that's okay.
and if someone goes,
it's not because you
were too much, or not enough,
it's just life passing through.
i wish i had known
that true friends will be shown,
in the people that stay,
when you feel all alone.
that being 'pretty' and 'cool'
is not all there is,
it is kindness, and love
that bring us closest.
i wish i had known

that being 'perfect', is not worth it,
and that what truly matters
isn't your grades, or your outfit.
what truly matters,
is that life feels exciting
that you wake up each day
ready for all it may bring.
oh i could go on,
with so many wishes,
but there's one last thing,
and it's not too ambitious,
stay a child.
for as long as you can.
for childhood only happens
once in a lifespan.
and soon you'll be grown
and sitting here like me,
writing what you wish you had known,
when you were young and carefree.

April 2021, London

there are things in life that will hit you so hard, you won't know how to stand back up again. but remember your courage, your bravery, your determination, that has gotten you through every challenge before. you may not know what the next step looks like, or how long it will take to get where you want to be. but know that every day you are here, breathing, something is changing, you are moving forwards, and one day you will stand up strong and see everything you overcame.

your fight is a show of light

when darkness comes,
and you can't see through,
remember these things
that have always been true.
that you have defeated
every cloud of rain,
that you have risen,
time and time again.
and that strength you had
will always be there,
and i know this challenge
feels so unfair,
but this is not the time
to lay down and give up,
for you were made to keep walking
and keep standing up.
and although you are tired,
there will come a day,
when you will be able
to stand up and say,
'look where i came from,
what i have fought through,
and if i can do it,
so can you'
and others will follow you
in your light,
and it will be worth
the longest fight,
for this is not a battle
for only yourself,
you are fighting for you,
and everyone else.

May 2021, London

in a year, you'll be in a new place. you'll have new thoughts and feelings, and maybe new problems too. but you'll have a years more experience in coping in your world and you'll have a years more strength gathered from picking yourself up and carrying on. everything changes. you don't need to decide who you are right now. in a years time you will look in the mirror and see someone you havn't seen before. and you may think you know who that will be, you know how everything is going to turn out. but every day your life takes a new path. a tiny turn in a direction you couldn't possibly foresee. so stay with it. you need to see who you become.

silence

let mountains hear your voice,
breaking as your secrets find daylight.
there is nothing more freeing,
than breaking your own silence.
and once you do,
vow to never be quiet again.

a story of recovery

what more do you want from me?
for i have no more to give.
do you want my friends too?
or my desire to live?
you just take and take
and give nothing back,
and with every defence
comes another attack.
you stole my years
of teenage dreams,
my holidays wasted
just following schemes.
i believed your lies,
that it would make me better,
and i followed your rules
to every last letter.
but instead i got tired,
miserable and weak,
i hoped it would change,
but it just got more bleak.
and i tried so hard
to get to the top.
but instead i fell ill,
and i just couldn't stop.
and 8 years later,
you still chat away,
telling me this lie and that,
saying it will all be okay,
if i just try again,
just one more go,
this time i'll be happy,
but this time i know,
all the promises you make

are empty when said,
and you will never be quiet
until i am dead.
so i am saying no.
that will not be my way
of living and breathing
day after day.
i see now there is no beauty
in starving the self,
for when you starve one thing
you starve everything else.
all the laughter, the joy,
the kindness, the tears
you thought you'd be stronger
but you're just haunted by fears.
no, not again,
with its momentary high,
then everything crumbles
and again you will try.
well i've stopped trying
to satisfy your goal,
for i have better things to do
than be in your control.
all those things you promised,
they never came,
but now i can find them,
as i'm done with this game.
for true happiness lies in friends,
in family & love,
in the deep rolling sea,
and the stars up above.
for this is the life,
that i wanted to know,
and now i've found it,
i won't let it go.

the shore

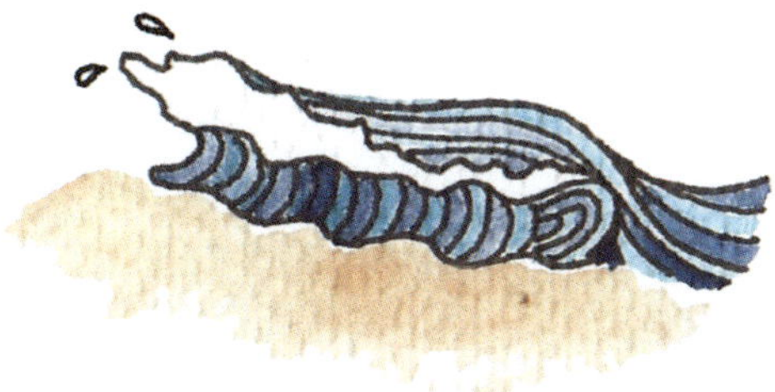

May 2021, London

you are more than your hard days. you are more than what people who didn't really know you, thought you could be. you are more than your past and you are more than the future you imagine for yourself. you are more than the thoughts you tell yourself and you are more than the hurtful things people have said to you. don't settle for the compromised version of yourself you may have become, out of fear of what happens if you really let yourself truly be everything and anything you can be. you must find that fighting spirit inside that knows and wants you to be more than who you are today.

thank you

i don't know how to say thank you,
when there aren't really words to explain,
the change in myself as you held the good, the bad,
my laughter and my pain.
i met you as a little girl,
so scared of the world around,
i didn't speak or use my voice,
and i couldn't hold my ground.
i know i was hard and slightly chaotic,
like a changeable stormy sea,
but you brought a boat and patiently waited
and sailed along side of me.
and gradually i learned that although i thought
i felt safer swimming on my own,
my arms were tired and i was out breath
from swimming all alone.
so there i was in this boat,
no idea what it would entail,
so scared of getting it very wrong,
so scared that i would fail.
but we kept on slowly sailing,
and the storms kept throwing me out.
but every time, i got back in,
and you held my hand throughout.
and overtime i learned to sail,
sometimes on my own,
but the sun would appear to make sure i knew,
i wasn't really alone.
and when the clouds turned darker,
and i knew a storm was on its way,
i knew to breath and be gentle,
for the storm will have its day,
but i am stronger than i thought i was,

and no storm is bigger than i,
i may be scared to sail on,
but the waves are never too high.
and what i've realised now,
is the strength that got me through,
wasn't given to me by other people,
it wasn't given by you.
you just showed me how to look and find,
what i always had inside,
you were a listener, a teacher, a parent, a mentor,
a trustworthy, gentle guide.
so i will keep on sailing,
the wind spurring me on to better days,
i'll miss you being beside me,
but the sun is out, and i'll be okay.

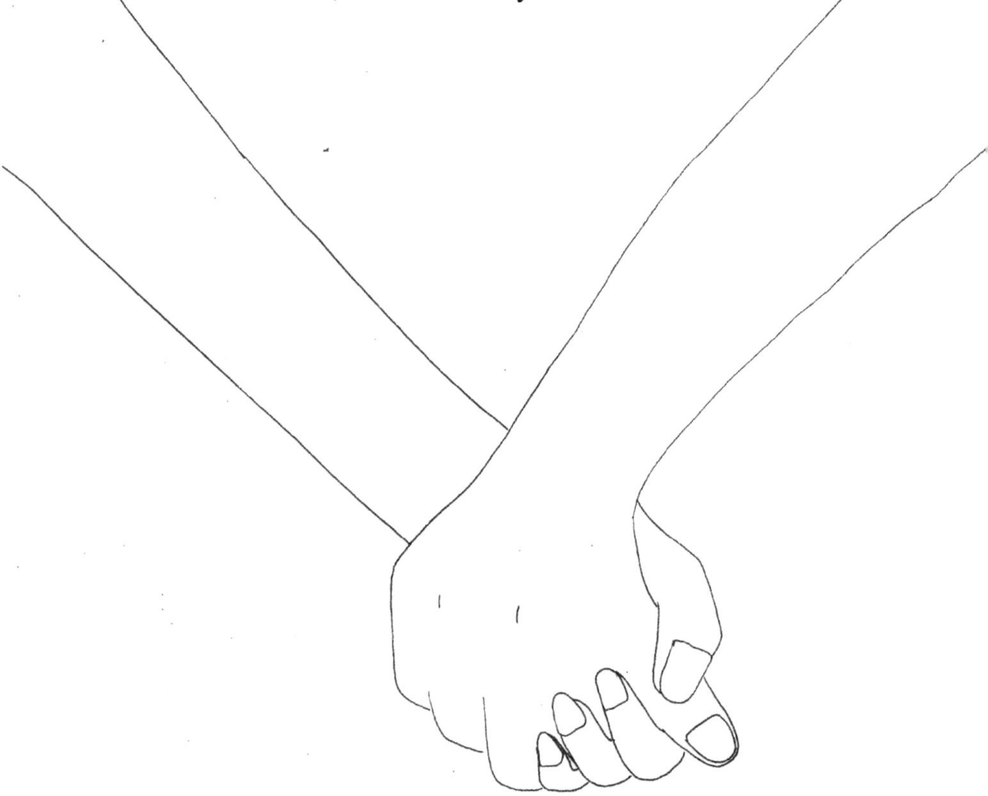

June 2021, London

not all heavy things are there to pull you down. some are there to help you realise how strong you are, to help you grow stronger wings, to fly even higher than before.

June 2021, London

sometimes it's not about who was wrong, or bad. something bad, hard, happened. you're not bad, they're not bad, it was just a bad thing. and that's hard, because we want to find someone to blame. but the world becomes a lot safer when we stop labelling people as 'bad' and 'good'. we instead become a world of fallible human beings, who hurt each other, and make mistakes, and sometimes we pull each other down. but if you let other people make mistakes, you can let yourself make mistakes too. no one, no matter how hard they try, can avoid making mistakes. but this is what unites us. every person has some good inside them. and when we come together, we have an unshakeable strength to stand together, to be together, in all our brokenness, and we finally see each other for who we are. imperfect and wonderful. complicated and brave.
hurt and healing. human.

June 2021, London

don't strive to be happy all the time. don't strive to do everything you think need to do. don't strive to be the best. don't strive to escape pain and heartbreak, for you will be running forever.

strive to make your hope unshakeable. strive to learn from everything. strive to know yourself right down to the core and strive to let the important people see you. and if you do this, you might find that you are already much further along than you think you are.

July 2021, London

beautiful things are medicine.

i don’t believe everything
happens for a reason, but
it seems in nature it does.
everything in nature,
whether simple, beautiful or
tragic, happens for a reason.
so when you feel lost for
answers, walk into the wild,
and remember, sometimes good
things have to break for better
things to fall together.

July 2021, Denmark

imagine if you already knew how incredible you are. imagine if every time you did something kind you remembered it just as much as the other person did. imagine if you could see yourself smile, could see yourself laugh, could feel the warm hug you gave to others, could hold your hand or look into your eyes.

you will never understand the impression you leave on this world. you will never fully comprehend what it means to love you. and that may sometimes make it easy for you to give up on yourself. to tell yourself stories about how you wouldn't be missed.

but if you loved yourself like others do, you would never let yourself go.

you can't wait for life not to be hard anymore

there are so many reasons,
so many excuses,
to just give up,
for there are too many bruises,
but this is when
you decide who you are,
to see all of the beauty,
not only the scar.
for there is beauty in heartbreak
and love in the ruins,
connection in pain,
and healing in bruises,
and one thing i wish,
i had known before,
is you can't wait for life,
to not be hard anymore.

August 2021, London

let go of who you thought you were meant to be. shed your skin. breathe into your bones and let your life fill your lungs. the journey is only just beginning.

August 2021, London

sometimes i wish i believed in god. so i could trust that this is all within his plan for me. that there is a reason.
maybe there is no reason. but there is a purpose. maybe there is no plan. but i will grow.
i will look back in five years time, and i will know why.

August 2021, London

are you holding onto that person who left you, letting them fill up every corner of your mind, just so you feel a little less alone? a little less empty?

sometimes torturing ourselves with someone's leaving is a way to make sure they never actually leave.

August 2021, London

some things may feel like they are trying to take you away from the strength and resilience you have to make it through this day, this week, this year, this life. you'll fall over, and you will expect yourself to not be able to get up again.
but you will stand back up, as you have done so many times before, because that is what you have inside you - an infinite ability to challenge and fight and live and breath, no matter the power of the difficult things.

you are more than what you expect of yourself. and one day you will have walked a path you didn't know you had within you, and you will look back, and despite yourself, you will feel proud. for there are some battles that just cannot be undermined.

and maybe, one day, you might even see it all laying behind you, and be thankful for the pain. for it gave
you power. power to keep changing, and moving into who you are today.

August 2021, London

to love and be loved.
that is all there is to it.

August 2021, London

we grew up being told that 'you can do anything as long as you try hard enough'.

one of the hardest pills to swallow is that sometimes no amount of trying can change the situation.

August 2021, London

there are three reasons as to why i am afraid of others;
the hurt they could cause.
the hurt i could cause.
the hurt they could find.

August 2021, London

grief, when you boil it down, is really just uncontainable love. filling you up and pouring out. but no where to go.

August 2021, London

sometimes i think we can become addicted to trying to make people love us when they're not supposed to love us. often we are surrounded by so many people who have that unquestionable, unshakeable love for us. and yet we don't see it. we seek love from people who aren't going to love us. because we like the challenge. the momentary high when it feels like we might just have won them over. love is called a drug for a reason. we become addicted to the highs and lows because it makes us feel alive in the way that constant, safe love, doesn't. and we break ourselves down in the process, because it will never be enough, we will never feel loved enough, because it was never meant to be that way. it is a hole that can never be filled because the love we are seeking in those people, doesn't exist.

and so the next obvious thing to say, is that we need to fill the hole up ourselves. and that is true, but it also comes with noticing how loved we already are. the love we became used to, the love we take for granted because it has always been there, it's become a blueprint of our life that we don't even notice anymore.

and it may be messy, and complicated, and not come in the forms we want it.

but it is there. you are so loved already. you don't need to convince someone to love you. someone who truly loves you will never make you feel like you need to win their love.

you cannot

if someone came up to me now, and said 'i want to die', how could i respond? could i tell them all the words that seemed so empty when i heard them myself? how can you convince someone that their pain is not as real as it seems? because that is a lie. the pain is just as real as it seems.

i could tell them an endless list of things to live for. their family, their friends, their children or future children.

i could tell them all the things they will miss out on, finding their first or second or third love, getting married, holding their baby.

i could tell them how incredible they are, how beautiful, how clever, how kind, how loving they are, how the world needs them to be here.

i would tell them all these things and i would know that they are all true.

but when it really comes down to it, there is one thing i would say.

'you cannot'.

for when the pain is searing through their veins they will hear nothing of what you say, it will sound like mythical stories and plans god made for other people, but they will be convinced it must not be for them.

you must tell them one simple word.

'no'.

you cannot. you must not. no matter what is going through your mind, and through your life, the only answer that will ever exist, is no.

you must live. no matter the pain, the grief, the sorrow, the loneliness, no matter the hopelessness and helplessness, you must live. you must hold on to see it get better.

there is only and will only ever be one answer.

you cannot.

August 2021, London

take me out of who i am,
bring me home, hand in hand.
show me how to love my soul,
piece me back together whole.
hold my words with delicate touch,
so i may never feel i am too much,
show me who i've always been,
help my heart be free and seen.

September 2021, London

it was a confusing way to live.
the more you loved me, the less i loved myself.

September 2021, London

sometimes i find myself wondering where i would be if that one thing or another, didn't happen. i look back over my past and i try and pick the moment where i could have stayed before everything changed.

the version of myself before i was here.

it can be tempting to want to go back. but then i realise it's a completely pointless exercise. because the version of my life i'm imagining, isn't my life. it isn't me. if i wasn't who i am now, i wouldn't have been who i was then. she only existed because i exist. i only exist because she existed.

a new version of myself turns up every day. and it is impossible to have one without having the thousands of others. so thank you, for being who you were. for allowing me to be who i am today.

September 2021, London

it's funny because the depression i have had has in some ways made me happier than i ever could be. because having been so low, in a place where there was nothing to hold onto and nothing to stay for, happiness is now even happier than before. and honestly, i wouldn't give that up for the world. i am so glad i know how special happiness is. i am so grateful i don't take it for granted.

September 2021, Denmark

i have discovered that if i don't prioritise myself, i am of no use to anyone else.

September 2021, Denmark

how many times have i heard the saying 'if you can't love yourself, you can't love someone else'?

i don't agree. of course you can love someone else. but i think it's those of us that love ourselves the least, that crave love from others the most. the sad thing is, when you don't love yourself, it doesn't matter how much love you receive, you will find it infinitely harder to hold onto it.

so if you want to feel loved, it starts with yourself.

November 2021, London

it's my birthday. i feel safe. i feel a kind of happiness that makes me realise how sad i've been. and that's really sad. i feel sad for younger me, i feel sad for the birthday spent in hospital, the birthday where my cake was a plate of dates and blueberries, the birthday spent alone at university, the birthday that kick started a three week breakdown, the birthday where i decided to stop eating, the birthday spent in treatment.

and then here we are today, on my 24th. the room feeling lighter than it ever has before. and i think about how only seven months ago i risked never seeing another birthday.

and how grateful i am that my story didn't end there. how amazing it is that i get to keep writing the book, sprawling the pages with laughter and tears and chaos. how happy i am that 24 isn't too late to start again. it's never too late. don't ever let it be too late.

and the thing is, what i have now, it isn't because someone swooped in to save me. it isn't because the world finally gave me the life i wanted. it isn't because my brain suddenly decided to give me a break.

it is because i realised that despite anything, *anything*, humans are made to live, made to fight, made to survive.

and that surviving can be frightening, when it involves staying for the pain and the grief, but it is *always* better than nothing. i no longer believe, that there is anything, that is worth giving up everything, for nothing.

November 2021, London

the world became mine when i allowed myself to be in it.

November 2021, London

i lost everything, and in that, i found what was left. myself.

a new story

you don't know me anymore
i may look the same
albeit my hair grew a little thicker
and my joints are a little tighter
my nails a little longer.
but i used to be a single plain
stretching out in the horizon
the sun set the same time
every single day.
you don't know about the ocean
that opened up inside me
how the world looks so different
through eyes that have seen a war.
how everything is shifting
like tectonic plates of earth
tsunamis sent across
the lands long deserted.
the storm and the calm
mixed up in all its glory
creating stories i have never seen
chaos and beauty,
intertwined, aligned.
i was blind to myself
and you were blind to me
but how should you have seen
when i could not see myself.
you don't know me anymore
and how happy i am for us
that we can both lose ourselves in the storm,
and find ourselves again.

I would like to express my deepest thanks to my mother, my father, to my beautiful sisters and brother, and the rest of my wide and wonderful family who have supported me on this life-long journey. Who have stayed with me through the toughest of times and done everything in their power to help me into the light, and who continue to share in all my happiness and laughter and love.

And to my extended family -- my extraordinary friends, who I wouldn't be here without. Who inspired me to be brave, to keep writing, and gave me the confidence to put my words and art into the world. Who have shown me unconditional love, and shown me what it truly means to not be alone.

And to all the wonderful humans I met on my journey, strangers who became unforgettable parts of my life, who gave me their time, who pushed me forwards, who gave me hope.

You have all taught me what it means to love, and be loved.

Printed in Great Britain
by Amazon

70925877R00076